SCHIRMER'S LIBRARY
OF MUSICAL CLASSICS

Vol. 1074

HANS SITT

Concertino

In E Minor

Op. 31

For Violin and Piano

(FIRST – THIRD POSITION)

ISBN 978-0-7935-3477-7

G. SCHIRMER, Inc.

DISTRIBUTED BY

7777 W. BLUEMOUND RD. P.O. BOX 13819 MILWAUKEE, WI 53213

Concertino

Hans Sitt. Op. 31

Allegro moderato

Violin

Piano

Tempo I

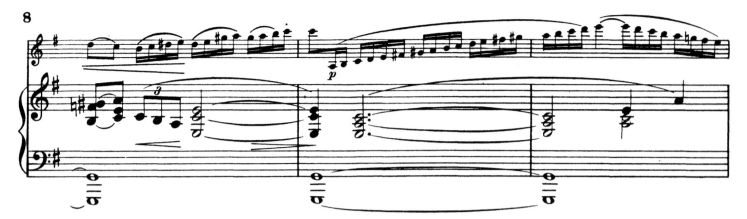

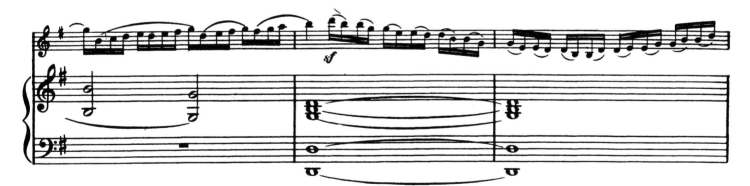

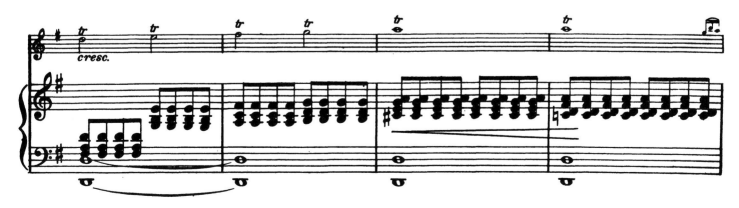

Animato

Andantino

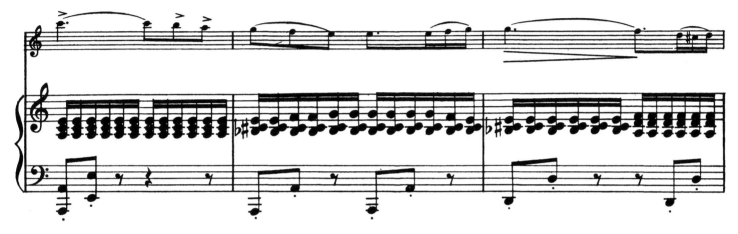

Concertino

Violin

Hans Sitt. Op. **31**

Printed in the U.S.A. by G. Schirmer, Inc.

Violin

Meno mosso

4

Tempo I

Violin

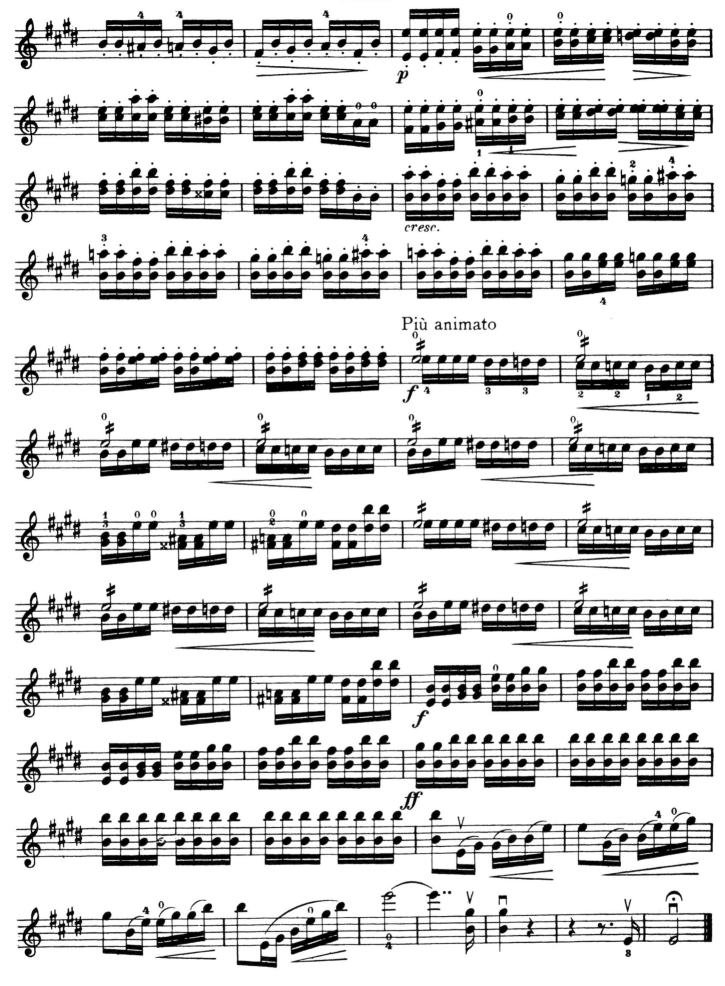

Allegretto

Più animato

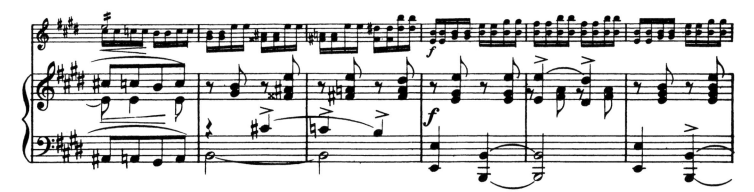